The Complete Field Guide to

Kitty Cat
Positions

To Carol —

I hope you sight
every position documented here!

Categorically
yours,

Linda
Miles

Published by Longmeadow Press, 201 High Ridge
Road, Stamford, CT 06904.

Cover designs by Betty Wilson and Linda Miles.

All illustrations for the text and covers were made
using Adobe Illustrator™ for Windows™.

Library of Congress Cataloging-In-Publication Data

Miles, Linda, 1947-
    The complete field guide to kitty cat positions /
by Linda Miles & Betty Wilson.—1st ed.
      p. cm.
    Includes indexes.
    ISBN 0-681-41788-9 : $6.95
    1. Cats—Humor. I. Wilson, Betty, 1953-   . II. Title.
PN6231.C23M54   1992
818'.5402—dc20   92-40530
                                        CIP

Printed in the United States of America

First Edition
0 9 8 7 6 5 4 3 2 1

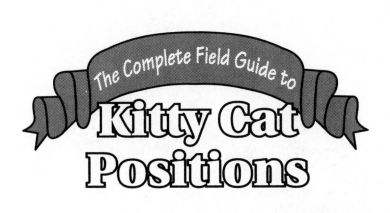

The Complete Field Guide to Kitty Cat Positions

by Linda Miles & Betty Wilson

LONGMEADOW
P   R   E   S   S

# Contents

Kitty Cat Positions

Personal Sighting
Record

Distribution of Kitty Cat Positions

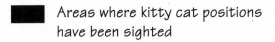

Areas where kitty cat positions
have been sighted

Areas where kitty cat positions
have not been sighted

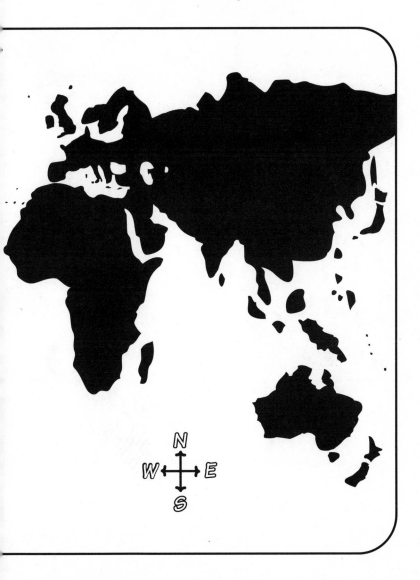

How To Use This Guide

No one can explain it to us. While legions of scientists through the ages have conducted in-depth research on millions of subjects, the science of Kitty Catology has lain neglected in the field. It seems university professors worldwide prefer to study the cognitive abilities of worms and the sex life of Brazilian toads instead of the familiar creatures that share their sofas and beds. It may be hard to believe, but this is the first official field guide on kitty cats to be published since Brubaker and Bottomley's monograph of 1879.*

Which is where you come in. Though this field guide presents the most complete record of documented sightings to date, the possibility remains that new positions will be discovered. Until now, amateur cat-watchers have had no official place to record, organize, and analyze their discoveries. This book provides the register wherein you can enter your findings.

---

* Brubaker, R. T. and Bottomley, N. L., *A Field Guide to Kitty Cat Habitats of South Central London*. Oxford: Olde Meadow Press, 1879.

1

Carry this guide around at all times so you can immediately identify and check off the positions you sight. As you come across new positions, use copies of the blank frame at the end of the book to record your findings.

We are interested in keeping at the forefront of this important research. Send us copies of your discoveries. If a follow-up book becomes necessary, we may want to include your scientific advancements. Send the documentation of your personal research to the address on page 115.

Incidentally, we are at work on another guide – *A Field Guide to Predator Cat Positions.* At present, Linda Miles crouches in a blind in northern Tanzania fending off tsetse flies and watching lions *(Felis leo)* approach giant catnip-filled mouse decoys. Betty Wilson is braving frostbite and avalanches in the Nepalese Himalayas as, sketchbook in hand, she tracks the elusive Siberian snow leopard *(Felis uncia)*. The book may be out by the turn of the century.

Meanwhile, we hope you appreciate the relative comfort and safety of your home as you make your own contributions to the study and science of feline positions.

Kitty Cat Positions

In the
Living Room

Meatloaf Kitty

(Felis casserolus)

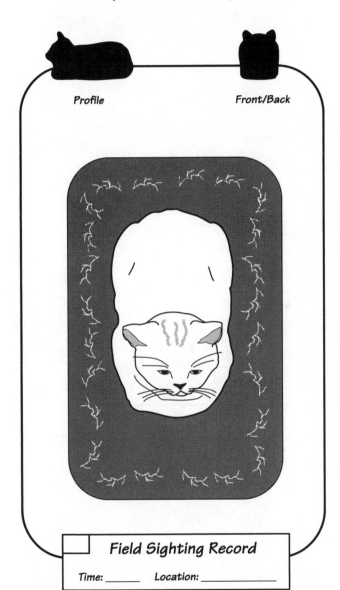

Profile   Front/Back

Field Sighting Record

Time: _____   Location: _____

Antimacassar Kitty

(Felis doilis)

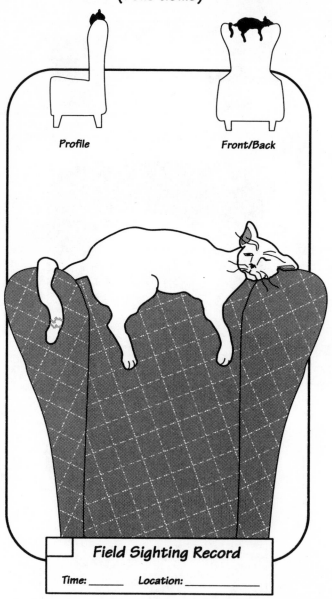

Profile

Front/Back

Field Sighting Record

Time: _____ Location: _____

Knickknack Kitty
(Felis porcelainus)

Profile

Front/Back

Field Sighting Record

Time: _____   Location: _____

Contortionist Kitty

(Felis twistis)

Profile

Front/Back

Field Sighting Record

Time: _____   Location: _____

See-No-Evil Kitty

(Felis innocenti)

Profile

Front/Back

Field Sighting Record

Time: _____   Location: _____

Gearshift Kitty

(Felis stickshiftus)

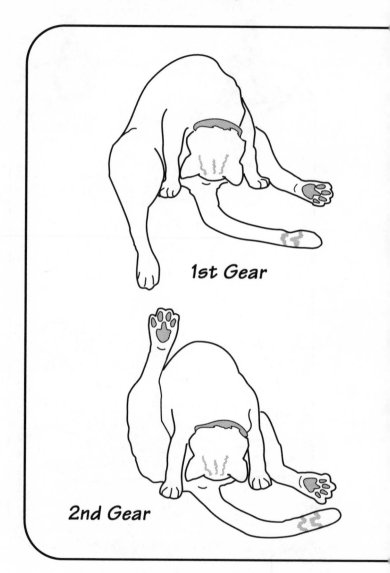

1st Gear

2nd Gear

3rd Gear

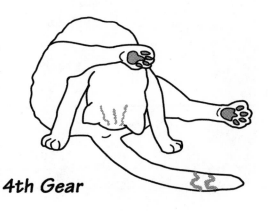

4th Gear

Frog Kitty

(Felis ribbitus)

Profile

Front/Back

Field Sighting Record

Time: _____   Location: _____

Newspaper Kitty

(Felis obstructus)

Profile   Front/Back

Cat Saves Master & Dog

Study Proves Cat Owners are More Intelligent

Field Sighting Record

Time: _____ Location: _____

Foot Pet Kitty

(Felis orthopedis)

Profile

Front/Back

Field Sighting Record

Time: _____   Location: _____

Slasher Kitty

(Felis remodelus)

Profile

Front/Back

SOLD!
DELIVER TO
RICK WALKER
555 GATO DR.

Field Sighting Record

Time: _____   Location: _____

Debutante Kitty

(Felis prissicus)

Profile   Front/Back

Field Sighting Record

Time: _____   Location: _____

Evil-Eye Kitty

(Felis moonis)

Profile

Front/Back

Field Sighti

Time: _____   Location: _____

Sneaky Paw Kitty

(Felis battus)

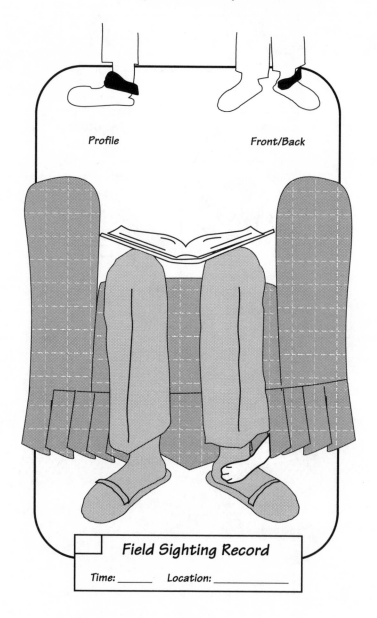

Profile   Front/Back

Field Sighting Record

Time: _____   Location: _____

Hot Dog Kitty

(Felis inabunnus)

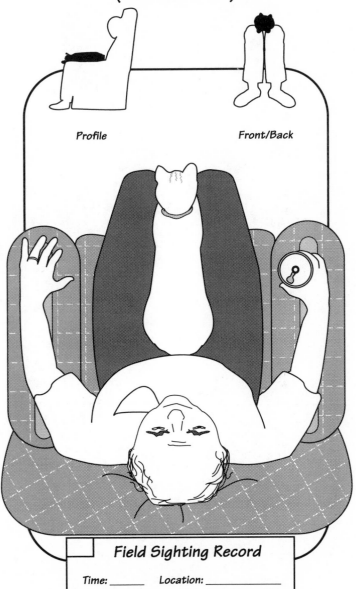

Profile

Front/Back

Field Sighting Record

Time: _____   Location: _____

Mozart Kitty

(Felis amadeus)

Profile   Front/Back

Field Sighting Record

Time: _____   Location: _____

Kitty Cat Positions

In the
Family Room

Hairball Kitty

(Felis upchuckus)

Profile

Front/Back

Field Sighting Record

Time: _____   Location: _____

TV Kitty

(Felis obscurus)

Profile

Front/Back

Field Sighting Record

Time: _____ Location: _____

Playtime Kitty

(Felis frolicus)

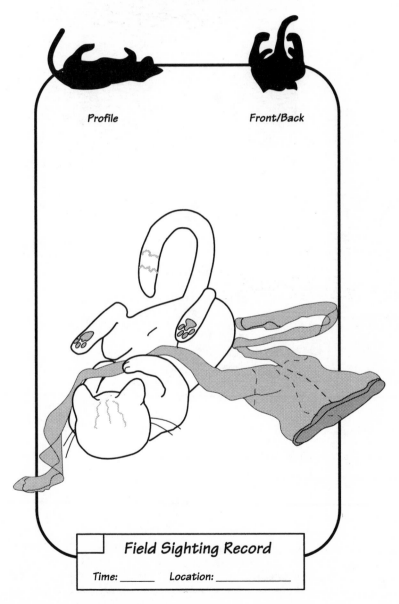

Profile   Front/Back

Field Sighting Record

Time: _____ Location: _____

Scuba Kitty

(Felis fishus)

Profile

Front/Back

Field Sighting Record

Time: _____   Location: _____

Insufferably Cute Kitty

(Felis cutsiepoous)

Profile

Front/Back

Field Sighting Record

Time: _____   Location: _____

Giftwrap Kitty

(Felis anniversarius)

Profile

Front/Back

Field Sighting Record

Time: _____ Location: _____

Indy 500 Kitty

(Felis streakus)

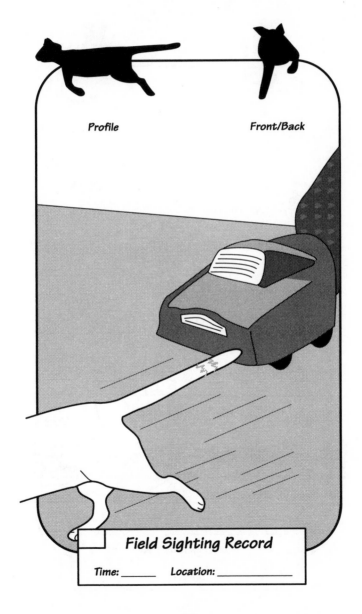

Profile

Front/Back

Field Sighting Record

Time: _____   Location: _____

Ragdoll Kitty

(Felis limpusraggis)

Profile

Front/Back

Field Sighting Record

Time: _____   Location: _____

Rigor Mortis Kitty

(Felis stiffis boardis)

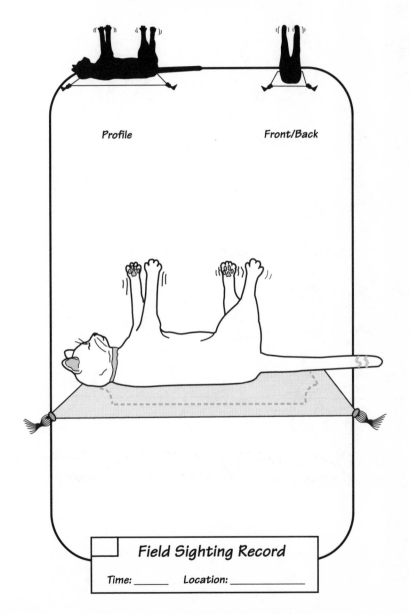

Profile

Front/Back

Field Sighting Record

Time: _____   Location: _____

Cyclone Kitty

(Felis chasatailus)

Profile

Front/Back

Field Sighting Record

Time: _____ Location: _____

Peopleweight Kitty

(Felis leadenlumpus)

Profile   Front/Back

Field Sighting Record

Time: _____   Location: _____

Wisdom Kitty

(Felis maharishii)

Profile

Front/Back

I Led 9 Lives

For Whom the Food Bell Tolls

How to Avoid Hot Tin Roofs

When bad things happen to good cats

The Complete Field Guide Positions

Field Sighting Record

Time: _____ Location: _____

Kitty Cat Positions

In the
Bedroom

Cowpie Kitty

(Felis cowpatticus)

Profile

Front/Back

Field Sighting Record

Time: _____   Location: _____

Eiffel Tower Kitty

(Felis landmarkus)

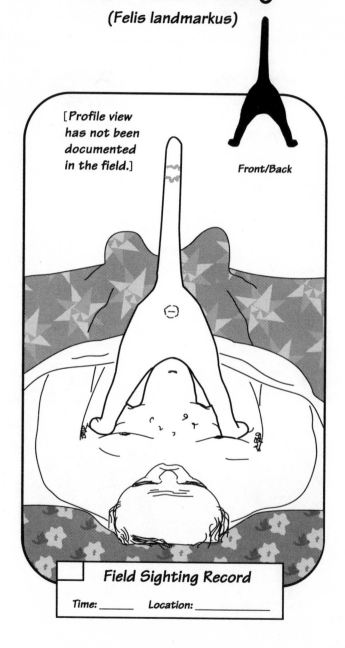

[Profile view has not been documented in the field.]

Front/Back

Field Sighting Record

Time: _____ Location: _____

Tête-à-Tête Kitty

(Felis proboscis frigidus)

Profile

Front/Back

Field Sighting Record

Time: _____   Location: _____

Pacifier Kitty

(Felis nursus)

Profile

Front/Back

Field Sighting Record

Time: _____   Location: _____

Undercover Kitty
(Felis spelunkis)

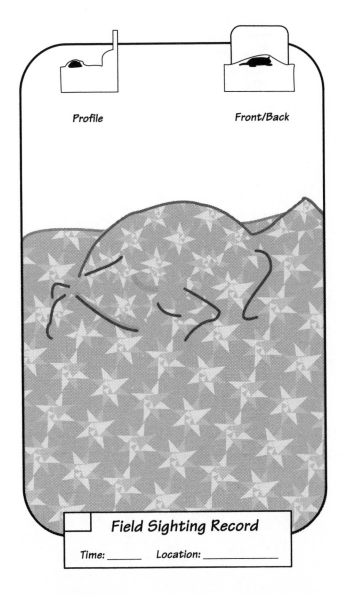

Profile

Front/Back

Field Sighting Record

Time: _____ Location: _____

Pillowmate Kitty
(Felis snoris)

Profile

Front/Back

Field Sighting Record

Time: _____ Location: _____

Triangle Kitty
(Felis isosceles)

Profile

Front/Back

Field Sighting Record

Time: _____ Location: _____

Wakeup Kitty
(Felis yawnis)

Profile

Front/Back

Field Sighting Record

Time: _____ Location: _____

44

Vulture Kitty

(Felis hoverus)

Profile

Front/Back

Field Sighting Record

Time: _____   Location: _____

Peek-a-Boo Kitty

(Felis boous)

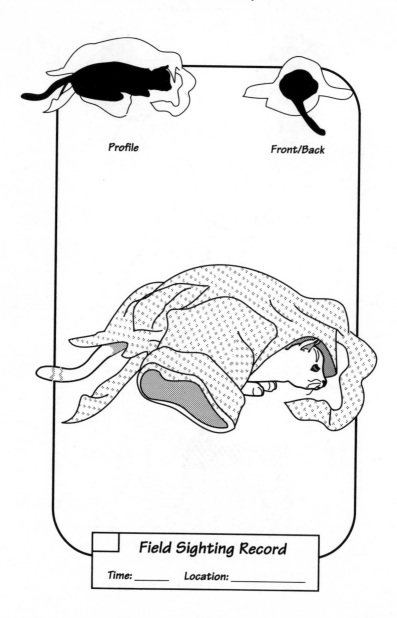

Profile

Front/Back

Field Sighting Record

Time: _____   Location: _____

Linen Closet Kitty
(Felis secludus)

Profile

Front/Back

Field Sighting Record

Time: _____   Location: _____

Masseuse Kitty

(Felis manipulatus)

Profile

Front/Back

Field Sighting Record

Time: _____ Location: _____

Mountain Goat Kitty

(Felis ibex)

Profile

Front/Back

Field Sighting Record

Time: _____ Location: _____

Catnip Kitty
(Felis addictus)

Profile

Front/Back

Field Sighting Record

Time: _____ Location: _____

Kitty Cat Positions

In the
Bathroom

Plumber Kitty

(Felis flushus)

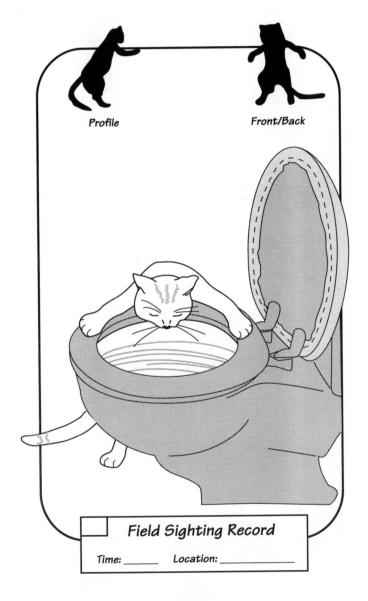

Profile

Front/Back

Field Sighting Record

Time: _____ Location: _____

Bathtime Kitty

(Felis escapus)

Profile

Front/Back

Kitty Suds

Field Sighting Record

Time: _____ Location: _____

Crybaby Kitty
(Felis meowis)

Profile

Front/Back

Field Sighting Record

Time: _____   Location: _____

Reach-For-It Kitty

(Felis assistis)

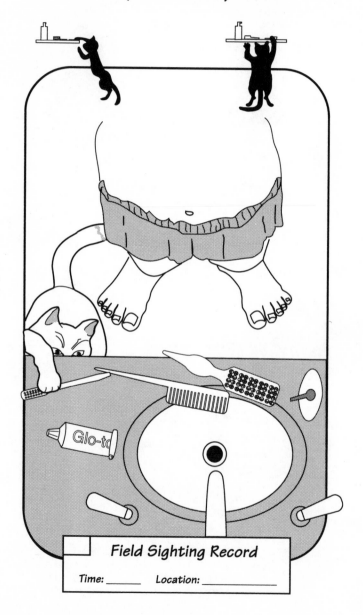

Field Sighting Record

Time: _____ Location: _____

Toilet Paper Kitty

(Felis dispensis)

Profile   Front/Back

Field Sighting Record

Time: _____   Location: _____

Hamper Kitty
(Felis snoopus)

Profile

Front/Back

Cowpie Kitty

(Felis cowpatticus)

Field Sighting Record

Time: _____   Location: _____

Kitty Cat Positions

In the
Home Office

Hacker Kitty

(Felis crashus)

Profile

Front/Back

and in consideration
of this complex law
let us consider the
infulence of a;lspe0
-q.........x--\\
--x xxxfYRAM[54
xxxxxklXELAsgyw
502=54=56

Field Sighting Record

Time: _____   Location: _____

Literary Kitty

(Felis eruditis)

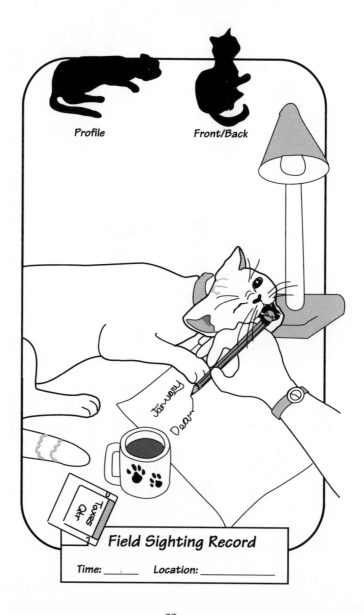

Profile

Front/Back

Taxes Qtr

Field Sighting Record

Time: _____ Location: _____

Watch-It-Fall Kitty

(Felis newtonis)

Profile

Front/Back

Paperwad Kitty

(Felis fetchis)

Profile

Front/Back

Field Sighting Record

Time: _____   Location: _____

Stretch Kitty

(Felis elasticus)

Profile   Front/Back

Field Sighting Record

Time: _____   Location: _____

Scratch Kitty

(Felis verminis)

Profile

Front/Back

Field Sighting Record

Time: _____   Location: _____

Kitty Cat Positions

In the
Kitchen

Paperbag Kitty
(Felis bagitis)

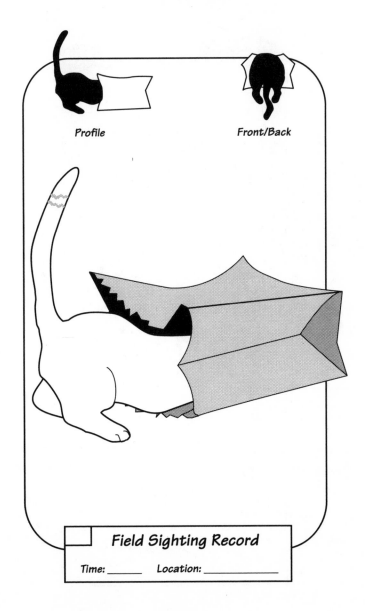

Profile

Front/Back

Field Sighting Record

Time: _____ Location: _____

Pantry Kitty

(Felis culinaris)

Profile

Front/Back

Field Sighting Record

Time: _____   Location: _____

Table Manners Kitty

(Felis sneakabitis)

Profile

Front/Back

Field Sighting Record

Time: _____ Location: _____

Tidy Kitty
(Felis sanitizus)

Post Breakfast Ablutions
Face/Ear Var.

Mid-Snack Ablutions
Front Paw Var.

Post Lunchtime Ablutions

Lower Back Var.

Post Dinnertime Ablutions

Inner Leg Var.

(Not to be confused with Gear Shift Kitty which is non-food related.)

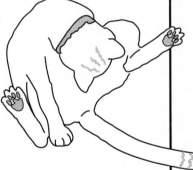

Field Sighting Record

Time: _____   Location: _____

Trash Can Kitty

(Felis scavengeus)

Profile

Front/Back

Field Sighting Record

Time: _____   Location: _____

Kitty Cat Positions

In the
Garage

Box Kitty

(Felis geometricus)

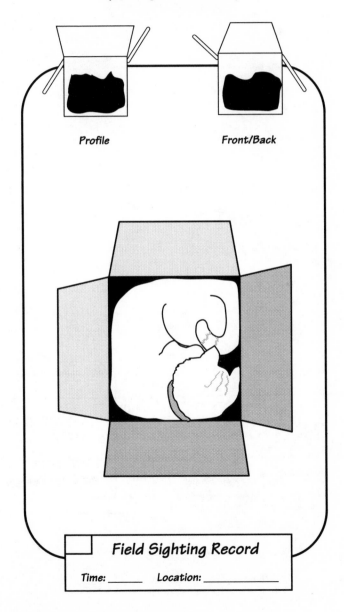

Profile   Front/Back

Field Sighting Record

Time: _____   Location: _____

Reverse Gear Kitty

(Felis reluctus)

Profile

Front/Back

**CoziComfort
Kitty Cat Carrier**

Field Sighting Record

Time: _____ Location: _____

Invisible Kitty

(Felis transparentis)

Profile

Top/Bottom

Field Sighting Record

Time: _____   Location: _____

Oilspot Kitty

(Felis mechanicus)

Profile   Front/Back

I ❤ Catrina

T R U C K

Classic
OLDBLUE
Kitty Cat Lover

Field Sighting Record

Time: _____   Location: _____

Kitty Cat Positions

In the
Desert

Sphinx Kitty
(Felis egyptus)

Profile

Front/Back

Field Sighting Record

Time: _____   Location: _____

Psycho Kitty

(Felis tyranntis)

Profile

Front/Back

Field Sighting Record

Time: _____   Location: _____

Centipede Kitty
(Felis truckinus)

Profile

Front/Back

Field Sighting Record

Time: _____   Location: _____

Dustbath Kitty

(Felis filthus)

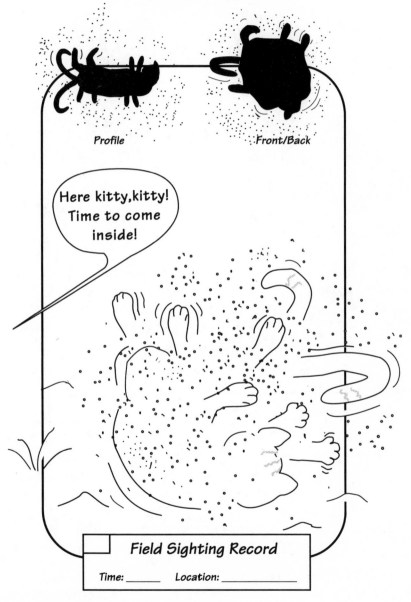

Profile

Front/Back

Here kitty,kitty! Time to come inside!

Field Sighting Record

Time: _____   Location: _____

Aerialist Kitty

(Felis equilibrius)

Profile

Front/Back

Field Sighting Record

Time: _____   Location: _____

Gangster Kitty

(Felis bullicus)

Profile

Front/Back

Field Sighting Record

Time: _____   Location: _____

Tinkle Kitty

(Felis numerus unus)

Profile

Front/Back

Field ~~ting~~ Record

Time: _____ Location: _____

Kitty Cat Positions

In the
Jungle

Poopoo Kitty

(Felis numerus duo)

Profile

Front/Back

Begonia foliosa

The Fun of Organic Gardening

Zinnia elegans

Field Sighting Record

Time: _____   Location: _____

Terminator Kitty

(Felis snuffusoutis)

Profile

Front/Back

Field Sighting Record

Time: _____ Location: _____

Pounce Kitty

(Felis strikus)

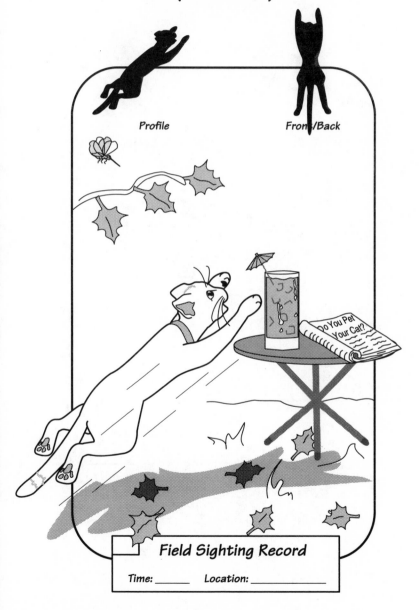

Profile

Front/Back

Do You Pet Your Cat?

Field Sighting Record

Time: _____   Location: _____

Casanova Kitty

(Felis amorous)

Profile

Front/Back

Field Sighting Record

Time: _____   Location: _____

Climber Kitty

(Felis cantgetdownus)

Profile

Front/Back

Field Sighting Record

Time: _____   Location: _____

Vegetarian Kitty

(Felis fiberis)

Profile

Front/Back

Field Sighting Record

Time: _____ Location: _____

Camouflage Kitty

(Felis concealus)

**Never sighted but
somehow sensed in the field.**

Leisure Kitty

(Felis ultralazicus)

Profile

Front/Back

Field Sighting Record

Time: _____   Location: _____

Kitty Cat Positions

On the
Veranda

Trod-Upon Kitty

(Felis guilt trippus)

Profile

Front/Back

Field Sighting Record

Time: _____   Location: _____

Guardcat Kitty

(Felis welcomis)

Profile

Front/Back

Field Sighting Record

Time: _____ Location: _____

Picky Kitty

(Felis finicus)

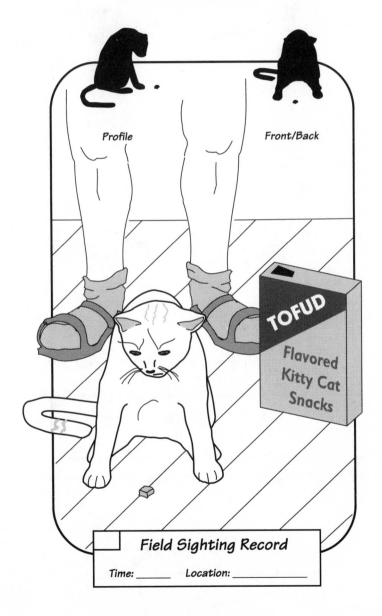

Profile

Front/Back

TOFUD

Flavored
Kitty Cat
Snacks

Field Sighting Record

Time: _____   Location: _____

Screen Door Kitty
(Felis suspendii)

Profile

Front/Back

Field Sighting Record

Time: _____ Location: _____

Scaredy Kitty

(Felis fraidicus)

Profile

Front/Back

Field Sighting Record

Time: _____ Location: _____

Contemplating-the-Cosmos Kitty

(Felis universalis)

Field Sighting Record

Time: _____   Location: _____

You can help us keep our scientific research
up-to-date. Please mail copies of your records
of newly discovered kitty cat positions to:

The Institute for Kitty Cat Research
P. O. Box 27644
Rancho Bernardo, CA 92198

_____

Common Name

_____

Latin Name

Profile   Front/Back

Field Sighting Record

Time: _____   Location: _____

Index of Common Names

Index of Latin Names

A

Felis addictus, 50
Felis amadeus , 20
Felis amorous, 100
Felis anniversarius, 28
Felis assistis, 56
Felis attackus, 18

B

Felis bagitis, 69
Felis blockadus, 72
Felis boous, 46
Felis bottomlesspita, 73
Felis bullicus, 93

C

Felis cantgetdownus, 101
Felis casserolus, 5
Felis chasatailis, 32
Felis concealus, 103
Felis cowpatticus, 37, 58
Felis crashus, 61
Felis culinaris, 70
Felis cutsiepoous, 27

D

Felis doilis, 6
Felis dispenseris, 57

E

Felis egyptus, 87
Felis elasticus, 65
Felis equilibrius, 92
Felis eruditus, 62
Felis escapus, 54

F

Felis fetchis, 64
Felis fiberis, 102
Felis filthus, 91
Felis finicus, 109
Felis fishus, 26
Felis flushus, 53
Felis fraidicus, 111
Felis frolicus, 25

G

Felis geometricus, 81
Felis guilt trippus, 107

H

Felis hoverus, 45

I

Felis ibex, 49
Felis ignoris, 89
Felis isosceles, 43
Felis inabunnus, 19
Felis innocenti, 9

L

Felis landmarkus, 38
Felis leadenlumpus, 33
Felis limpusraggis, 30

M

Felis manipulatus, 48
Felis maharishii, 34
Felis mechanicus, 84
Felis meowis, 55
Felis moonis, 17

N

Felis newtonis, 63
Felis numerus duo, 97
Felis numerus unus, 94
Felis nursus, 40

O

Felis obscurus, 24
Felis obstructus, 13
Felis orthopedis, 14

P

Felis porcelainus, 7
Felis prissicus, 16
Felis proboscis frigidus, 39

R

Felis reluctus, 82
Felis remodelus, 15
Felis ribbitus, 12
Felis rolus-polus, 74

S

Felis sanitizus, 76-77
Felis scavengeus, 78
Felis secludus, 47
Felis sneakabitis, 75
Felis snoopus, 58
Felis snoris, 42
Felis snuffusoutis, 98
Felis spelunkis, 41
Felis stickshiftus, 10-11
Felis stiffis boardis, 31
Felis streakus, 29
Felis strikus, 99
Felis suspendii, 110

T

Felis tailmashus, 71
Felis transparentis, 83
Felis truckinus, 90
Felis twistis, 8

Felis tyranntis, 88

U

Felis ultralazicus, 104
Felis universalis, 112-113
Felis upchuckus, 23

V

Felis verminis, 66

W

Felis welcomis, 108

Y

Felis yawnis, 44